THEY SAID IT!

200 of the funniest sports quips & quotes collected from the pages of *Sports Illustrated*

Edited by David Fischer

Kingston, New York Sports Illustrated™ New York, New York

For information about permission to reproduce sections of this book, please write to:
Permissions
Total Sports Publishing
100 Enterprise Drive
Kingston, New York 12401
www.TotalSportsPublishing.com

ISBN 1-892129-83-3

They Said It was prepared by
Bishop Books, Inc.
611 Broadway
New York, New York 10012

Printed in Canada

ADAGES
& APHORISMS

Jeff Van Note, Atlanta Falcons center, told that his club's draftees had potential:

"Potential is a French word that means you aren't worth a damn yet."

July 2, 1984

Earl Strom, NBA referee:

"Officiating is the only occupation in the world where the highest accolade is silence."

June 13, 1977

Andre Agassi, tennis player, assessing his career so far:

"I've only scratched the iceberg."

July 9, 1990

George Armstrong, Toronto Maple Leafs scout who is part North American Indian, on the controversy over Indians as the subject of a team insignia:

"When I was playing, it wasn't the Black Hawks' crest that bothered me. It was Bobby Hull's slapshot."

March 13, 1972

Earl Warren, Chief Justice of the United States:
"I always turn to the sports section first. The sports page records people's accomplishments; the front page has nothing but man's failures."

July 22, 1968

Bill Lee, Red Sox lefthander, asked why southpaws are always depicted as flakes:
"What do you expect from a northpaw world?" May 29, 1978

Glenn Healy, New York Rangers netminder, on whether any goalies observe the NHL's limit on the size of leg pads:
"Sure, they're all in the minors."

December 16, 1996

Paul Hornung, asked why he got married at 11 a.m.:
"Because if it didn't work out I didn't want to blow the whole day."

February 27, 1967

John Brodie, asked why a million-dollar quarterback has to hold the ball for field goals and extra points:
"Well, if I didn't, it would fall over."

January 18, 1971

Johnny Kerr, former NBA player and coach, now a broadcaster:
"If a coach starts listening to the fans, he winds up sitting next to them."

June 11, 1979

Scott Skiles, Orlando Magic guard, dismissing the fans' booing of him:
"Basketball is like church. Many attend but few understand."

February 15, 1993

Mickey Rivers, Texas Rangers outfielder, explaining why he opposed an early-season players' strike:
"There are more games in the second half than the first."

May 19, 1980

Mike Macfarlane, Kansas City Royals catcher, after K.C. beat the Oakland A's 3–1 on only one hit:
"That was a maximization of a minimization of hits."   April 27, 1992

Doug Dieken, Cleveland Browns offensive tackle, asked how he expected to be remembered after he retires:
"Holding . . . No. 73." February 27, 1984

Otis Birdsong, New Jersey Nets guard, enumerating the three certainties of life:
"Death, taxes and my jump shot." April 18, 1983

A.J. Foyt, on suggestions that stock cars be slowed down by mechanical alterations:
"Race cars are built to run fast. If you want to slow up, all you have to do is lift that foot." April 10, 1967

Bear Bryant, Alabama football coach, on the role of athletics on the campus:

"It's kind of hard to rally 'round a math class."

April 2, 1973

Tony La Russa, youthful White Sox manager, on baseball wisdom imparted by veteran major league pilot Chuck Tanner:
"When I first became a manager, I asked Chuck for advice. He told me, 'Always rent.' " August 27, 1984

Ralph DeLeonardis, minor league umpire, after a disputed call:
"I blew it the way I saw it." September 27, 1993

Don Zimmer, the Chicago Cubs' manager, after his team went 4–4 on a recent road trip:
"It just as easily could have gone the other way." May 28, 1990

Jim DeShaies, Minnesota Twins pitcher, on ignoring baseball tradition and changing his seat in the dugout during teammate Scott Erickson's no-hitter:
"I think everybody gets caught up in superstitions. But I don't put much stock in them—knock on wood." May 16, 1994

Edgar Jones, San Antonio Spurs forward, on his energetic style:
"I can play a little faster than full speed." April 23, 1984

Lou Duva, veteran boxing trainer, on the spartan training regimen of heavyweight Andrew Golota:
"He's a guy who gets up at six o'clock in the morning regardless of what time it is." December 23, 1996

Irving Rudd, publicist, on his relationship with boxer Thomas Hearns:
"There's nothing I wouldn't do for him, and there's nothing he wouldn't do for me, and that's how it's been for 10 years now. We've done nothing for each other."
November 7, 1988

Ron Meyer, Indianapolis Colts coach known for his malapropisms, shrugging off his bold decision to start rookie Jeff George at quarterback:
"It isn't like I came down from Mount Sinai with the tabloids."
September 24, 1990

Rocky Lockridge, journeyman boxer, after stopping Mike Zena in a junior lightweight fight:
"I ain't been nowhere, but I'm back." June 26, 1989

Willie Pep, former featherweight champion, on reports of his death:
"Naw, I'm not dead. I ain't even been out of the house."
June 27, 1988

Ron Davis, former Minnesota Twins reliever who had a knack for giving up late-game homers, on the boos he still hears at appearances in the Twin Cities:
"When it's 10 years later and they still hate you, that's what you call charisma." February 20, 1995

Jack McDowell, Chicago White Sox pitcher, acknowledging that the public knew very little about him:
"In fact, I don't know a lot about me." October 22, 1990

Fran Curci, University of Kentucky football coach, in the weekly UK football letter:
"Both teams used basically the same offense, which is based on having the ball." October 28, 1974

Darrell Royal, Texas football coach:
"Football doesn't build character. It eliminates the weak ones."
April 16, 1973

Duane Thomas, Dallas Cowboys running back, asked if he had an IQ:
"Sure I've got one. It's a perfect 20-20."   July 26, 1971

Dennis Rappaport, boxing manager, on why he was reluctant to comment about his relationship with fighter Thomas Hearns:
"I don't want to tell you any half-truths unless they're completely accurate."   October 8, 1990

Jack Mildren, New England Patriots defensive back, on his familiarity with the offensive tendencies of his old team, the Colts:
"They know I know and I know they know I know, but I don't know how much I know."   December 16, 1974

Don Smith, Atlanta Falcons defensive end,
on the expected return of fellow defensive end
Jeff Yeates for a 13th NFL season:

"The thing that's kept Jeff around is his longevity."

May 28, 1984

Mike Shaw, publicity director of the NBA's Buffalo Braves, on the termination of coach Jack Ramsay's contract:

"He's not fired. He's just not rehired."   May 17, 1976

New York Yankees first baseman Don Mattingly before facing the Mets' Dwight Gooden in an exhibition game:

"His reputation preceded him before he got here."   April 3, 1989

Gene Stallings, Texas A&M football coach, hearing TCU coach Abe Martin say his team's main strength was its lack of weakness:

"I guess that makes our main weakness lack of strength."

                                                            October 24, 1966

George Steinbrenner, New York Yankees owner, evaluating his ace pitcher:
"David Cone is in a class by himself with three or four other players."
September 23, 1996

Junior Ortiz, Cleveland Indians catcher, after going 0 for 3 while playing with his left contact lens in his right eye and his right lens in his left eye:
"When the pitcher threw a fastball low and outside, it looked like a fastball high and inside."
June 8, 1992

Ralph Kiner, New York Mets broadcaster, to hot outfielder Daryl Boston:
"You have really solidified the Mets' centerfield problem."
October 8, 1990

Marques Johnson, Seattle SuperSonics broadcaster, calling the action during a game against the Sacramento Kings:

"Corliss [Williamson] is going to go the amphibious route, changing from the right to the left hand."
January 12, 1998

Bobby Ussery, on Reflected Glory, a Kentucky Derby favorite:

"He may be a late starter, but he's an early finisher."
April 3, 1967

Dave Aldana, motorcycle racer, on what it's like to fall off a bike at 150 mph:

"It's kind of like tumbling around inside a giant clothes dryer."
October 27, 1975

Derek Hardy, head golf pro at Snee Farm Country Club in Mount Pleasant, S.C., and Beth Daniel's teaching pro, on why he charged $1,000 for a single lesson yet offered a series of 13 lessons for $140:

"If you expect a miracle, you should expect to pay for one."

July 26, 1971

Zane Smith, Boston Red Sox lefty, on the previous week's rumors that he would be left off the postseason roster:

"I'm not blind to hearing what everybody else hears."

October 9, 1995

Barry Beck, New York Rangers defenseman,
asked who started a bench-clearing brawl in the
previous week's Stanley Cup playoff game against
the Los Angeles Kings:

"We have only one person to blame, and that's each other."

April 20, 1981

Buck (Tombstone) Smith, after being accused of padding his welterweight record (110-2-1, 81 knockouts) with a bum-of-the-month schedule:
"But I'm not fighting one bum a month. I'm fighting three or four."
June 8, 1992

Don Ott, of the evangelically oriented Athletes in Action basketball team, explaining the club's 29-point loss to UCLA after beating Oral Roberts by 29 in its previous game:
"You might say they did unto us as we did unto others."
January 24, 1983

Litterial Green, Georgia guard, after the Bulldogs beat Georgia Tech 66–65:
"It's not how good you are when you play good. It's how good you are when you play bad. And we played pretty good, even though we played bad. Imagine if we'd played good." December 30, 1991

Dennis (Oil Can) Boyd, Boston Red Sox pitcher, on not being told about a bomb threat against the plane that took his team from spring training to Baltimore:
"They keep me pretty much in the dark about everything. If it had blown up, I wouldn't have known anything about it." May 1, 1989

Tug McGraw, Philadelphia Phillies relief pitcher, the proud owner of a 1954 Buick:
"I like it because it plays old music."
April 26, 1982

Willie Hernandez, Detroit Tigers reliever, "apologizing" for dumping a bucket of ice water on Detroit Free Press columnist Mitch Albom:
"A lot of people make mistakes. I believe I made a good mistake."
March 14, 1988

Mark Snow, a skinny, 6' 10" New Mexico basketball player, assessing his talents in a speech to the school's booster club:
"Strength is my biggest weakness."
April 6, 1981

Chico Resch, the loquacious New York Islanders goaltender:
"If I wasn't talking, I wouldn't know what to say." January 14, 1980

Yogi Berra, reminiscing during a TV interview about New York Yankees battery mate Don Larsen's perfect game in the 1956 World Series:
"It's never happened in World Series competition, and it still hasn't."
November 5, 1990

Bum Phillips, ex-NFL coach, on how he's spending his retirement:
"I ain't doing a damn thing, and I don't start until noon."
March 20, 1995

Torrin Polk, University of Houston receiver, on his coach, John Jenkins:

"He treats us like men. He lets us wear earrings."

October 14, 1991

Pete Incaviglia, Texas Rangers outfielder, arguing that baseball players aren't overpaid:

"People think we make $3 million and $4 million a year. They don't realize that most of us only make $500,000." April 2, 1990

Luis Polonia, California Angels outfielder recently acquired from the New York Yankees, criticizing his former team for using him mostly as a pinch hitter and designated hitter:

"The Yankees are only interested in one thing, and I don't know what that is." May 14, 1990

Otto Graham, just before the Cleveland Browns and the Cincinnati Bengals met for the second time ever:
"It will be a typical Browns-Bengals game." October 19, 1970

Howard Cosell, discussing San Francisco quarterback Tony Owens:
"I'm impressed by the continuity of his physical presence."
November 25, 1974

Davey Johnson, Baltimore Orioles manager, on the possibility of his benching Cal Ripken Jr.:
"He's no different from anyone else, except that he's doing something no one else has ever done or ever will do." September 29, 1997

Ulf Dahlen, a center from Sweden who's with the New York Rangers, when asked about the possibility of Soviet players joining the NHL the next season:

"I don't like it. We can't let foreigners take our jobs."

March 28, 1988

Davey Johnson, soon-to-be-former Cincinnati Reds manager, assessing the Atlanta Braves lineup before his club was swept from the playoffs:
"They've got a lot of guys you fear the most."   October 23, 1995

Detroit Tigers catcher Bill Freehan, who had been hit 20 times by pitched balls that season:
"They ought to stop it before somebody gets hurt."
September 2, 1968

Rich Makoff, basketball coach of the Crossroads School in Santa Monica, Calif., on the selection of Donald McCleary to a high school All-America team:

"He's only five-eleven, but he outjumped guys six feet tall all year long." May 22, 1978

Doc Medich, New York Yankees, on pitching to Henry Aaron:

"It certainly was a great thrill. And someday he can tell his grandchildren that he hit against me." July 7, 1975

Mickey Rivers, Texas Rangers designated hitter:
"We'll do all right if we can capitalize on our mistakes." April 23, 1984

Ralph Kiner, Hall of Famer and New York Mets broadcaster, on relief pitcher Steve Bedrosian, who was recently traded from the Philadelphia Phillies to the San Francisco Giants:
"All of his saves have come during relief appearances." July 3, 1989

Ralph Kiner, New York Mets broadcaster, during a telecast:
"All of the Mets' road wins against Los Angeles this year have been at Dodger Stadium."
July 17, 1989

George Chemeres, Seattle boxing promoter, asked to explain what he meant by his term, "Half-a-David":
"You know, a Half-a-David is one of those legal papers you prove things with."
March 8, 1971

Chris Dundee, fight promoter:
"I'd love to be a procrastinator, but I never seem to get around to it."
June 18, 1973

Harry Caray, World Series telecast announcer, describing the sound of the crowd as Bob Gibson neared his record 17 strikeouts:

"The groan is audible. It can also be heard." October 14, 1968

Anthony Mason, Charlotte Hornets forward, claiming that the Hornets' offense works best when run through him in the low post:

"I don't need the ball to score." April 6, 1998

Mike Gottfried, Kansas football coach, on learning that the odds against his Jayhawks winning the Big Eight title were 100 to 1:

"Who's the one guy who thinks we can do it?" September 10, 1984

Pete Vuckovich, Pittsburgh Pirates pitching coach, after being ejected from a game against the St. Louis Cardinals for arguing from the dugout with first base umpire Randy Marsh:

"I was a victim of circumcision."

June 2, 1997

Bill Pulsipher, lefthanded pitcher for the New York Mets Triple A club in Norfolk, Va., on his request to be called up or traded:

"What does it hurt to ask? All they can say is yes or no, and I already know the answer."   May 18, 1998

Antawn Jamison, North Carolina star, on his decision to leave school early for the NBA:

"There's not much more to accomplish, other than maybe winning a national championship."   May 4, 1998

Leon Wagner, asked how he feels about the Cleveland Indians platooning him in leftfield:

"I'm pretending this pontooning ain't happening. When I don't play I pretend there's no game. It makes spring training go faster."

April 10, 1967

Yogi Berra, Yankees manager, asked if first baseman Don Mattingly had exceeded expectations this season:

"I'd say he's done more than that."

September 24, 1984

Brian Reese, North Carolina forward:
"This is a great school. Look at all the alumni who are in the NBA."

December 2, 1991

Mike Tyson, heavyweight boxing champion, explaining why, after reading Tolstoy novels during his three-year prison term, he now reads comic books:
"I'm not as deep and complicated as people think."

September 16, 1996

Vernon Maxwell, Houston Rockets guard, when asked by his coach, Don Chaney, to give a one-word description of his performance this season:
"Up and down."

February 17, 1992

Yogi Berra, New York Yankees immortal, reminiscing about his baseball career to the 1998 Little League World Series champions from Toms River, N.J.:
"If I had to do it all over again, I'd do it all over again."

September 14, 1998

John Pinone, Villanova center, on his style of basketball:
"I use intelligence to the best of my ability." January 24, 1983

Mike Riordan of the Washington Bullets, asked if second-year star Phil Chenier could be compared to the flamboyant Earl (The Pearl) Monroe:
"No, he's more unnoticeable than Earl." December 18, 1972

Terry Bradshaw, on demands the banquet circuit and his TV announcer's job have made on him since retiring from the NFL:
"When you're unemployed, you have to work all the time."

September 17, 1984

Yogi Berra, Mets manager, after receiving a check made out to "Bearer" for his appearance on Jack Buck's pregame show in St. Louis:
"How long have you known me, Jack? And you still don't know how to spell my name."

August 21, 1972

WITH ALL DUE RESPECT

Jim Killingsworth, Texas Christian basketball coach, of Tulsa guard Paul Pressey:

"He's quick enough to play tennis by himself."

March 15, 1982

Eddie Mathews, a batting instructor for the Atlanta Braves, on how you help Henry Aaron:
"By staying away from him." May 3, 1971

Phil Garner, Milwaukee Brewers manager, on Seattle Mariners fireballing lefthander Randy Johnson, who beat Milwaukee despite throwing a wild pitch, hitting two batters and striking out only three:
"Even when he's below average, he's above average." May 26, 1997

Lee Trevino, on Raymond Floyd's scheduled debut on the Senior PGA Tour:
"He'll be tougher than a 50-cent steak." December 28, 1992

Don Paul, former Los Angeles Rams linebacker, on shaking hands with Hall of Fame running back Hugh McElhenny, an erstwhile opponent:
"That's the first time I ever touched him." December 19, 1994

Jake LaMotta, having married for the sixth time, commented on his best man, Sugar Ray Robinson:
"He was the best man in our fights, too." July 7, 1986

Terry Francona, Philadelphia Phillies manager, on San Francisco Giants outfielder Marvin Benard, who was 12 for 18 against the Phils in one series:
"If he goes to arbitration, he should take us with him."
August 17, 1998

Johnny Miller, observing that he was happy not to be paired with Jack Nicklaus in the closing round of the Masters:

"That man makes you feel sort of insuperior."

April 26, 1971

Cal Stoll, University of Minnesota football coach:
"We finally got Nebraska where we want them—off the schedule."

August 25, 1975

Alvan Adams, Phoenix Suns center, accepting the NBA Rookie of the Year trophy:
"I'd like to thank coach John MacLeod, my teammates for making me look so good and, mostly, David Thompson for going to the ABA."

May 24, 1976

Dizzy Dean, recalling Bill Terry, the hardest hitter he ever faced:
"He once hit a ball between my legs so hard that my centerfielder caught it on the fly backing up against the wall." May 28, 1973

Roger Clemens, Boston Red Sox pitcher, when asked to name baseball's three most dangerous hitters:
"Robin Yount in the first, Robin Yount in the fourth and Robin Yount in the seventh." February 21, 1994

Paul Mirabella, Milwaukee Brewers pitcher, describing a towering home run the Oakland A's Jose Canseco hit off him:
"The homer had a crew of four and a meal on it." June 11, 1990

John Kerr, Chicago Bulls TV commentator and former NBA player and coach, on how he'd guard Kareem Abdul-Jabbar:
"I'd get real close to him and breathe on his goggles." May 3, 1982

Robin Roberts, Hall of Fame pitcher, describing his greatest All-Star Game thrill:
"When Mickey Mantle bunted with the wind blowing out in Crosley Field." July 24, 1978

Bobby Murcer, Chicago Cubs rightfielder, after facing Phil Niekro, the Atlanta Braves' knuckleballer:
"Trying to hit him is like trying to eat Jell-O with chopsticks."
September 11, 1978

*Don Maloney, New York Rangers wing,
revealing his New Year's resolution:*

"To get as many goals this year as Wayne Gretzky got last week."

January 11, 1982

Lester Hayes, Los Angeles Raiders cornerback, after playing against the Eagles' scrambling quarterback Randall Cunningham:
"He must shower in Vaseline."   December 15, 1986

Chi Chi Rodriguez, discussing Jack Nicklaus' infrequent tournament appearances:
"He's the only golfer in history who has become a living legend in his spare time."   March 20, 1978

Billy Crystal, comedian, telling peripatetic San Antonio Spurs coach Larry Brown during a roast how he used to idolize Brown when the two were at Long Beach (N.Y.) High together:

"I walked like you. I talked like you. I even moved four times."

February 13, 1989

Tom Paciorek, Seattle leftfielder, after striking out on three pitches against Yankee Ron Guidry:

"Of what I saw of him, he was unhittable, unbeatable and unthinkable. I might have been more impressed if I had seen more of his stuff."

May 21, 1979

Steve Kerr, Cleveland Cavaliers guard, after Michael Jordan said he could score 70 or 80 points against the Cavs with guard Craig Ehlo out of the lineup:
"I take that as a personal insult. I can hold him to 65 on any given night." April 20, 1992

Doug Buffone, Chicago Bears linebacker, on Fran Tarkenton's retirement:
"I haven't hit him yet, and now I never will." June 25, 1979

Tony Lema, after spending a couple of days at Arnold Palmer's house:
"I got lost in the vault." September 14, 1964

Montreal outfielder Clyde Mashore, on how to stop Pittsburgh slugger Willie Stargell:
"Buy a seat in the upper deck and play one of your outfielders there."
July 5, 1971

Colonel Edmund Edmondson, executive director of the U.S. Chess Federation, on the rule allowing each player in the Fischer-Spassky matches three delays for illness:
"Bobby Fischer's opponents usually get ill."
December 25, 1972

Steve Young, San Francisco 49ers quarterback, formerly of the Tampa Bay Bucs and the USFL's Los Angeles Express, on why he was attending the showing of the 49ers' highlights film:
"This is the first time I've played for a team that had a highlight film."
July 20, 1987

Dave Winfield, Angels outfielder, on hitting in front of newly acquired Dave Parker in the batting order:
"You're going to hear pitchers saying, 'Nobody told me there'd be Daves like this.' "
April 15, 1991

Don Zimmer, Texas Rangers manager, summoned to the phone on May 7 after his team snapped a 12-game losing streak with a 1–0 win over the Red Sox:
"Is this President Reagan calling?"
May 31, 1982

Wren Blair, Pittsburgh Penguins president, asked if Ken Schinkel was an interim coach:
"Aren't all coaches interim coaches?"
April 12, 1976

Kenny King, Oakland Raiders running back, on the effect of the NFL's new ban on the use of stickum by pass receivers:
"You'll still see great catches. They just won't be made with the elbows."
February 10, 1982

Rocky Bridges, manager of the minor league Salem (Va.) Buccaneers baseball team, when asked by a waiter if he wanted escargots—snails—as an appetizer:

"I prefer fast food."

June 19, 1989

Joe Niekro, Houston Astros 21-game winner in 1979, asked how he expected to pitch in the upcoming season:
"Righthanded."
April 28, 1980

Walter Payton, explaining why he wouldn't watch Monday Night Football:
"It makes as much sense as a secretary going home and spending her nights typing."
June 1, 1981

Rod Gilbert, New York Rangers right wing, asked whether hockey fights are faked:
"If they were faked, you would see me in more of them."
May 8, 1967

Willie Nelson, country singer, asked what par is on a golf course he recently bought near Austin, Texas:

"Anything I want it to be. For instance, this hole right here is a par-47—and yesterday I birdied the sucker."

March 16, 1981

Chi Chi Rodriguez, making light of the fact that he was closing in on the $1 million mark in career earnings as a golf pro:
"The problem is, I'm already over $2 million in spending."

May 9, 1983

Norm Charlton, Philadelphia Phillies pitcher, on having a triple major—in political science, religion and physical education—while at Rice University:
"If I can't talk you out of it or preach you out of it, I'll beat you out of it."

June 5, 1995

Mike Tomczak, Chicago Bears quarterback, divulging the name of the new formation the team had added for quarterback Doug Flutie:
"The sawed-off shotgun." November 24, 1986

Butch Alder, Purdue football player, when asked how his conversion in spring practice from linebacker to center was going:
"It's a snap." June 8, 1981

Ralph Campbell, one of the Hogettes, the unofficial male Washington Redskin cheerleaders who dress up as women, on his group's wardrobe:
"Our designer is Calvin Swine." January 21, 1991

Sammy Lilly, out-of-work NFL cornerback who had just interviewed for a job at a nuclear power plant in Georgia, after getting a call to play for the Los Angeles Rams:

"I'm thrilled about this. I'm glowing right now."

October 12, 1992

Danny Sullivan, Indy Car driver, after his car collided with ones driven by Scott Brayton, Scott Goodyear and Scott Pruett at the Detroit Grand Prix:
"I was just hoping to get away Scott-free." June 29, 1992

Cliff Stoudt, who advanced from No. 3 quarterback to No. 2 with the Pittsburgh Steelers when Mike Kruczek was traded:
"I've graduated from clipboard to headset." September 8, 1980

Frank Broyles, Arkansas athletic director, when asked if he would still like his football coach, Ken Hatfield, if the team went .500 this year:
"Sure I would. I'd miss him, too." September 8, 1986

The Kansas City Royals' 5' 4" Freddie Patek, on how it feels to be the shortest player in the major leagues:

"A heckuva lot better than being the shortest player in the minor leagues."
July 19, 1971

Jack Haley, Chicago Bulls rookie center, on his NBA debut, in which he played one minute and didn't score:

"I'll always remember it as the night Michael Jordan and I combined for 52 points."
December 12, 1988

World B. Free, Cleveland Cavaliers guard, after teammate Cliff Robinson sank a three-point shot at the final buzzer to beat Detroit 114–112 in overtime:
"That shot was so good, for a moment I thought I took it."

February 20, 1984

Ken Avery, Cincinnati Bengals linebacker, asked if anyone called him a sissy because he studied ballet:
"If they did, I'd stomp 'em and do a pirouette on their heads."

November 25, 1974

Earl Bruce, Ohio State football coach, on his 6' 4", 282-pound—with size 16 feet—offensive tackle Mark Krerowicz:

"He doesn't shine his shoes, he drives them through a car wash."

September 24, 1984

Ray (Boom Boom) Mancini, WBA lightweight boxer, recalling a recent White House visit with President Reagan:

"It's like meeting Santa Claus. You go in, shake his hand, have your picture taken and then you leave."

August 30, 1982

Len Dawson, the Kansas City Chiefs' 38-year-old quarterback, on the speed he displayed in scrambling for 21 yards in two carries against Denver:
"I may be faster. I'm more frightened than I used to be."

October 22, 1973

Mike Johnson, 5' 9", 165-pound Western Michigan defensive back, asked how he was physically able to make 56 tackles during the previous season:
"I'm so small, blockers just run right by me and look for someone bigger to hit."

November 6, 1972

Julius Boros, 57-year-old golfer, insisting he planned to continue playing occasional tour events:
"Retire? Retire to what? I already fish and play golf." July 4, 1977

David Brenner, comedian:
"I don't like to watch golf on television. I can't stand whispering."
May 2, 1977

Rodney Dangerfield, comedian:
"I went to a fight the other night and a hockey game broke out."
September 4, 1978

Neil Bonnett, stock car driver, explaining why he had a 300-horsepower motor on his lightweight, 19-foot fishing boat:
"You hook a bass at 100 miles per hour and it takes the fight right out of him."
October 25, 1982

Al Conover, Rice University football coach, on his snappy new pair of alligator shoes:
"I took them home and put them in the closet. Guess what? They ate my Hush Puppies."
September 23, 1974

Paul Householder, Cincinnati Reds outfielder who hit .211 the previous season, after confirming that he'd become engaged on New Year's Eve:
"With the kind of year I had, I'm ready to try anything."

January 24, 1983

Tony Dungy, former NFL defensive back, asked if he felt biorhythms influenced the outcome of games:
"I think your biorhythms are going to be better against San Francisco than they are against Pittsburgh." November 10, 1980

Roger Staubach, Dallas Cowboys quarterback, preparing to speak at a football dinner:

"I keep waiting for Mike Ditka and Bill Truax to bring in the words."

March 6, 1972

Dennis Awtrey of the Philadelphia 76ers on the team's red, white and blue uniforms, which include stars and stripes:

"When we play a bad game, it's like desecrating the flag."

December 6, 1971

Pete Rose, on the way his salary had gone up:

"With the money I'm making, I should be playing two positions."

June 20, 1977

Karl Mecklenburg, Denver Broncos veteran, on being shifted in recent years from noseguard to defensive end to inside linebacker to outside linebacker:
"I'm moving right up the evolutionary ladder."   August 6, 1990

Abe Lemons, Oklahoma City basketball coach, on how he came within two strokes of winning a car at a golf tournament:
"It was a hole-in-one contest and I had a three."   July 7, 1986

Joe Paterno, Penn State football coach, explaining how a player named Lincoln Lippincott III ever came to Penn State:
"He was looking for Princeton and got lost."   November 7, 1966

Eugene Lockhart, a linebacker traded by the Dallas Cowboys to the New England Patriots, while cleaning out his locker:

"It's a cold business—a cold, cold business. And it's even colder in New England."

May 13, 1991

Bob Brue, PGA Senior golfer:

"I used to play golf with a guy who cheated so badly that he once had a hole in one and wrote down zero on the scorecoard."

April 22, 1991

Marcellus Wiley, former defensive end at Columbia, a school more noted for academics than football, on taking the intelligence test at the NFL scouting combine:
"All of a sudden a lot of guys wanted to sit next to me."

April 21, 1997

Pete Rose, Phillies first baseman, after a plane circled Philadelphia's Veterans Stadium trailing a sign apparently meant for him and signed "Luv, Christy":
"I'm hard to reach on the phone."

May 25, 1981

Bob Froese, New York Rangers goalie, after fans at Madison Square Garden showered the ice with plastic mugs given to them as a promotion:

"I'm just glad it wasn't Machete Night."

April 10, 1989

Frank Coppenbarger, Philadelphia Phillies clubhouse manager, as a load of dirt was delivered to groundskeepers at Veterans Stadium:
"All of the old dirt was on Lenny Dykstra's uniform."   July 23, 1990

Bill Walton, on where he might play if he became an NBA free agent:
"Right now, I've eliminated Teheran and Three Mile Island."
May 7, 1979

Elvin Hayes, 6' 10" Washington Bullets forward, asked in a hotel lobby if he was a basketball player:
"No, I clean giraffe ears."   May 24, 1976

Tim Wood, Indianapolis high school senior, who broke the world record for consecutive sit-ups with 15,525 in 10 hours, asked what he wanted to do when he finished:

"Go to the bathroom."
April 9, 1973

Representative Joseph Moakley (D., Mass.), after lunching at the White House with Boston Marathon winner Bill Rodgers:

"It's good to have a guy running in my district that I don't have to worry about."
May 14, 1979

TEAM CHEMISTRY

Claudell Washington, explaining why it took him four days to show up after being traded by the Texas Rangers to the Chicago White Sox:
"I overslept."
June 5, 1978

Tim McCarver, the Philadelphia Phillie who caught all of Steve Carlton's games:
"When Steve and I die, we are going to be buried in the same cemetery, 60' 6" apart."
June 6, 1977

Ron Shumate, Southeast Missouri State basketball coach, on his team's shooting accuracy:
"It was so bad the players were giving each other high fives when they hit the rim."
March 29, 1982

Butch van Breda Kolff, former NBA coach, explaining why he prefers his present job with the New Orleans Pride of the Women's Basketball League:
"The timeouts smell a lot better."   January 5, 1981

Rick McCutcheon, ex-starter on the University of Minnesota basketball team after switching to Arizona State because of an "impossible situation":
"If I'm going to be unhappy, I might as well be unhappy where it's warm."   September 23, 1974

Yinka Dare, the New Jersey Nets center, who was still looking for his first career assist after 45 games:
"I'm not going to rush it. I'm not going to force it."   March 4, 1996

Monte Clark, former Detroit Lions coach,
on how to relate to today's players:

"The key to this whole business is sincerity. Once you can fake that, you've got it made."

September 1, 1997

Lew Burdette, Angels pitcher, asked about a batted ball which bounced off his leg and into the glove of teammate Joe Adcock:

"This wasn't my best assist. I once started a double play with my forehead."
August 22, 1966

Bob Uecker, Milwaukee Braves rookie, who had hit one homer and was rooming with Eddie Mathews:

"Between me and my roommate, we've hit 400 major league home runs."
March 18, 1963

Buck Williams, New Jersey Nets forward, explaining why he averaged barely one assist a game in 1982:

"I knew those guys were out there. I just didn't know where."

May 3, 1982

Tippy Martinez, Baltimore Orioles relief pitcher, asked how he expected to be affected by the trade to Oakland of fellow reliever Tim Stoddard, who weighs 250 pounds:

"There will be more food for everybody."

March 12, 1984

Roger Erickson, Yankees pitcher, announcing his retirement after being demoted to Columbus with assurances that he was part of the parent team's future:
"I don't want to be in your future. It's frustrating enough being in your present."
May 2, 1983

Gordon King, New York Giants 6' 6", 275-pound tackle, explaining why rookie Joe Morris, a 5' 7" running back, was a welcome addition to the team:
"He leaves plenty of room in the huddle."
August 30, 1982

Sterling Hitchcock, former New York Yankees pitcher then with the Seattle Mariners, on whether he missed pinstripes:
"Polyester is polyester."   June 3, 1996

Derrick Coleman, the New Jersey Nets forward, on why he turned down an invitation to hunt with teammate Jayson Williams:
"I'm not going hunting with anyone who plays the same position as me."
                                                                February 21, 1994

Dick Butkus, Hall of Fame middle linebacker, on his reputation for playing dirty:
"I never set out to hurt anybody deliberately unless it was, you know, important. Like a league game or something."   August 31, 1987

COACHES

Bear Bryant, divulging his favorite play:
"It's the one where the player pitches the ball back to the official after scoring a touchdown." February 20, 1978

Denny Crum, University of Louisville basketball coach, addressing attendees at the team's tip-off luncheon:
"First I'd like to welcome my assistant coaches . . . all 2,000 of you." October 19, 1992

Bill Yeoman, University of Houston football coach, on 5' 9" Cougar quarterback Gerald Landry:
"If he was 6' 2", he'd be All-America. Of course, if he was 6' 2", he'd be at Southern Cal."
June 11, 1984

George Raveling, Washington State basketball coach, one of the few African-American coaches in major college sports:
"When the athletic director said I should recruit more white players to keep the folks in Pullman happy, I signed Rufus White and Willie White."
March 10, 1980

Frank Layden, coach of the then hapless Utah Jazz, to a fan who had just called a referee a fool during a meaningless late-season game with the almost-as-hapless Kansas City Kings:

"Who are you calling a fool? You paid to watch this."　May 10, 1982

Dave Bristol, the San Francisco Giants manager, addressing his struggling team:
"There'll be two buses leaving the hotel for the park tomorrow. The two o'clock bus will be for those of you who need a little extra work. The empty bus will be leaving at five o'clock."　May 12, 1980

Hugh Durham, Georgia basketball coach, on the SEC's new 45-second clock:
"That won't be a factor for us. We'll either shoot the ball or throw it away by then."
December 13, 1982

Bill Foster, University of Miami basketball coach, on his players' jitters the first time they practiced in game uniforms:
"They threw up enough bricks during warmups to build a condominium."
December 2, 1985

Charlie Just, women's basketball coach at Bellarmine College in Louisville, on his team's inexperience:

"We're so young, we've decided to dress only seven players on the road. We're pretty confident the other five can dress themselves."

December 2, 1996

Mike Fratello, Atlanta Hawks coach, on being named vice president of the basketball team and gaining a seat on the board of directors:

"What that means is that the vote to fire me will never be unanimous."

September 8, 1986

*Don Nelson, Golden State Warriors coach, on his frontcourt duo of 7' 4",
230-pound Ralph Sampson and 7' 6", 225-pound Manute Bol:*
"We call them the Thin Towers."   December 5, 1988

*Jerry Tarkanian, University of Nevada, Las Vegas, basketball coach, on how he
prepares his team for games at Wyoming, where the elevation is 7,165 feet:*
**"I try to tell our guys that the altitude isn't that bad because we're
playing indoors."**   April 6, 1981

Don Osborn, Pittsburgh Pirates pitching coach:
**"The only thing wrong with our pitchers is they all have to pitch the
same night."**   May 24, 1976

Al Bianchi, coach of the Seattle SuperSonics, describing his young NBA club:
"This team is so aggressive we might foul out in warmups."

October 30, 1967

David McWilliams, Texas Tech football coach, whose team threw 72 passes in a spring game, when asked how many of those passes were completed:
"We worked on throwing in the spring. We'll work on catching in the fall."

August 18, 1986

Earl Weaver, Baltimore Orioles manager, when told by slump-ridden outfielder Al Bumbry that he was about to go to chapel services:
"Take your bat with you."

May 7, 1979

Billy Tubbs, Oklahoma's basketball coach:

"This year we plan to run and shoot. Next season we hope to run and score."

November 24, 1980

Lou Holtz, the then new football coach at Minnesota, whose team was much scored against the previous season:
"Any time your defense gives up more points than the basketball team, you're in trouble."
March 27, 1984

Kevin O'Neill, Tennessee basketball coach, on the depth of his team, which had been plagued by injuries:
"Our bench is kind of like a video store late on Saturday night. There aren't a lot of choices."
February 27, 1995

Lou Rymkus, coach of the defunct Akron Vulcans, asked when he knew his team was in financial trouble:
"When we couldn't get our uniforms out of the cleaners."

October 9, 1967

Tim Capstraw, Wagner College basketball coach, on the cultural makeup of his team:
"We have black players, white players, a Mormon and four Yugoslavians. Our toughest decision isn't what offense or defense to run, but what type of warmup music to play." December 30, 1991

Tom Moore, The Citadel's then new football coach, promising to give the Bulldogs a pass-oriented offense:

"Our running game's going to consist of running on the field and running off the field."   May 16, 1983

Barry Switzer, football coach at Oklahoma, asked whether he would stick with the wishbone:

"Well, since we're 54–3–1 with it, I suppose we will."   April 5, 1976

Dan Reeves, Atlanta Falcons coach, on the series of grudge matches on his team's schedule, including one against the Denver Broncos, his former team:
"I just hope we can do some vendetting." August 11, 1997

John McKay, Tampa Bay Buccaneers coach, wondering whether the injured Lynn Cain of Atlanta would be ready to play against Tampa Bay:
"Let me know if Cain is able." September 14, 1981

Tom Landry, commenting on the fact that he was the only coach the Dallas Cowboys ever had:
"That's one way to look at it. The other is that I haven't had a promotion in 21 years." February 16, 1981

Penn State football coach Joe Paterno, following a glowing introduction by former NFL coach Dick Vermeil:
"After that eulogy, the least I should do is drop dead."

December 28, 1992

Leon Wagner, Cleveland outfielder, on why manager Joe Adcock hadn't been using Rocky Colavito and him:
"Because we have no faults. Joe loves to correct faults, and that left us out. I've been trying to find a flaw that Joe could work on so that I could play more."

May 22, 1967

ZINGS
& ARROWS

Randy Cross, veteran 49ers center, choosing his words carefully as he announced his retirement:
"I'm not a boxer. I'm only going to do this once." January 30, 1989

Rich Donnelly, Pittsburgh Pirates third base coach, on retired pitcher Bob Walk's new job in the broadcast booth:
"Maybe now he'll get a complete game." March 21, 1994

Jeff Feagles, New England Patriots punter, on his junior college team, the Scottsdale (Ariz.) Community College Artichokes:
"We were known as the Chokes for short." October 31, 1988

Steve Alvarez, ABC sportscaster, on Ohio State's mammoth offensive linemen:
"When they go into a restaurant, they don't look at a menu. They get an estimate."
November 13, 1989

Lou Camilli of the Cleveland Indians:
"Maybe they ought to change our name to the Cleveland Light Company. We don't have anything but utility men."
July 26, 1971

Walt Garrison, former Dallas Cowboys running back, asked whether coach Tom Landry ever smiled:
"I don't know. I only played there nine years."
May 19, 1980

Gary Smith, Vancouver Canucks goalie, discussing 5' 5" teammate Bobby LaLonde:

"He'd be great in a short series."
April 21, 1975

Johnny Kerr, Chicago Bulls announcer, on 7' 4", 290-pound Utah Jazz center Mark Eaton:

"If you go to the movies with him, you get in for half price."
July 10, 1989

Pete Carril, Princeton basketball coach, on why he wouldn't move freshman Steve Goodrich from center to forward:

"He has the shooting range. What he doesn't have is the making range."

January 16, 1995

Johnny Bench, Cincinnati Reds broadcaster, on the wide-legged stance of the Phillies' lanky Von Hayes:
"He looks like a pair of pliers."
August 15, 1988

Don Meredith, former Dallas quarterback, on Cowboys coach Tom Landry:
"He's a perfectionist. If he was married to Raquel Welch, he'd expect her to cook."
September 10, 1979

Doc Medich, Texas Rangers pitcher, on the time-consuming ritual of twitches and stance adjustments that the Indians' Mike Hargrove goes through each time he steps into the batter's box:
"He's a one-man four-corner offense."
May 10, 1982

Tom Heinsohn, on fellow former Celtic Chuck Connors, who left basketball and went on to star in the TV series The Rifleman:
"Chuck went from the worst shot in the East to the best shot in the West."
November 24, 1986

Bob Brenly, San Francisco Giants catcher, on the outrageous wardrobe of teammate Kevin Mitchell:
"He's the only guy I know who does his clothes shopping at the San Diego Zoo. He puts five animals on the endangered species list with one outfit."
November 9, 1987

Doug Dieken, Cleveland Browns offensive tackle, at a roast for Houston Oilers defensive end Elvin Bethea, a 14-year veteran:

"Elvin is so old he had to use a jumper cable to get started last year."

May 24, 1982

Matt Elliott, Michigan center and the last player picked in the 1992 NFL draft, on Ohio State linebacker Alonzo Spellman, the Chicago Bears' first-round selection:

"Physically, he's a world-beater. Mentally, he's an eggbeater."

May 11, 1992

George Will, author and pundit, on football:

"It combines the two worst things about American life. It is violence punctuated by committee meetings."

July 30, 1990

Jimmy Demaret, after golfing with Bob Hope:
"Bob has a beautiful short game. Unfortunately, it's off the tee."

May 14, 1979

Martina Navratilova, on Andre Agassi, who passed up Wimbledon to rest:
"It's like a football player who skips the Super Bowl because he has to get ready for training camp."
July 16, 1990

Dan Quisenberry, discussing the control problems of another Kansas City Royals pitcher, Renie Martin:
"Some people throw to spots, some people throw to zones. Renie throws to continents."

April 13, 1981

Lynn Gottschalk, a volunteer driver at the ATP Championships in Cincinnati, to Andre Agassi, who balked at leaving the gate at the airport in northern Kentucky before security arrived:
"Andre, it's 11 p.m. and you're in Kentucky. Unless you've been on *Hee Haw* recently, no one's going to mob you." September 30, 1990

Garry Shandling, comedian, noting that lava from a Hawaiian volcano was traveling three feet an hour:
"That's one rush Jim Plunkett could avoid." December 15, 1986

Gary Player, on Lee Trevino's physique:
"If he didn't have an Adam's apple he'd have no shape at all."

July 31, 1972

Johnny Unitas, shrugging off news that Oakland quarterback Dan Pastorini had demonstrated his throwing prowess by heaving a football from a hotel parking lot to a sixth-floor balcony:
"His receivers were on the second floor."

August 25, 1980

Marty Springstead, American League umpire, on former Baltimore Orioles manager Earl Weaver:

"The way to test the durability of a Timex watch would be to strap it to his tongue."
April 23, 1984

George Raveling, Washington State basketball coach, on Indiana's Bobby Knight:

"He's the kind of guy who would throw a beer party and then lock the bathroom door on you."
April 23, 1979

Roger Craig, San Francisco Giants manager, extolling the determination of paunchy pitcher Don Robinson:
"His heart is as big as his stomach." July 2, 1990

Tex Cobb, whose beating at the hands of WBC heavyweight champion Larry Holmes prompted Howard Cosell to decide to stop announcing boxing:
"I'd go 15 more rounds with Holmes if I thought it would get Cosell off football broadcasts." May 30, 1983

Steve Spurrier, Florida football coach, telling Gator fans that a fire at Auburn's football dorm had destroyed 20 books:
"But the real tragedy was that 15 hadn't been colored yet."

December 2, 1991

Greg Haugen, anticipating his lightweight bout against Pernell (Sweet Pea) Whitaker:
"When I get done with Sweet Pea, he'll be Split Pea." January 9, 1989

Charles Barkley, 250-pound Philadelphia 76ers forward, on the advantages of playing alongside newly acquired 255-pound Rick Mahorn:
"It means people will be able to see I don't have the biggest butt in the league."
November 27, 1989

Alex Hannum, Oakland Oaks basketball coach, on the American Basketball Association's red, white and blue ball:
"The only place a ball like that belongs is on the end of a seal's nose."
October 21, 1968

Bill Muir, offensive line coach at SMU, on his team's lack of aggressiveness:
"If the meek are going to inherit the earth, our offensive linemen are going to be land barons."
May 10, 1976

Joe Vitt, former Baltimore Colts strength coach, discussing his boyhood career ambitions:
"I wanted to do two things—be a coach or be in the circus. With the Colts, I had a little of both."
October 25, 1982

Dan Quisenberry, Kansas City Royals relief pitcher, on what the slumping '84 Royals had to do to win:
"Our fielders have to catch a lot of balls—or at least deflect them to someone who can."
May 28, 1984

Don Knodel, Rice basketball coach, on one of his slow players:
"He has difficulty getting to where he knows he ought to be."
December 18, 1972

Emile Francis, coach and general manager of the New York Rangers, on the condition of the rink in Madison Square Garden:
"I've seen better ice on the roads in Saskatchewan."
March 6, 1972

Beano Cook, a publicist for CBS Sports and an ardent football fan, after baseball commissioner Bowie Kuhn gave the 52 former Iranian hostages lifetime major league baseball passes:
"Haven't they suffered enough?"

June 29, 1981

Oscar Robertson, Cincinnati Royals basketball star, when asked what he thought of Wilt Chamberlain getting $250,000 a year from the Philadelphia 76ers:
"Man, what could he get if he could shoot free throws!"

October 30, 1967

Bonnie Blair, speed skater and Sullivan Award nominee from Butte, Mont., when asked what outfit she will wear to the Sullivan dinner in March to avoid being overshadowed by glamorous sprinter and fellow nominee Florence Griffith Joyner:

"I don't know, but I'm sure not going to find it in Butte."

January 16, 1989

Roger Maltbie, the NBC golf analyst, after watching former tennis great Ivan Lendl hit five balls into a water hazard on the 18th hole of a celebrity golf tournament:

"Grass isn't his best surface."

January 8, 1996

Doug Russell, who beat the then unpopular Mark Spitz in the 100-meter butterfly at Mexico City in 1968, on Spitz' seven gold medals at Munich:
"It could have happened to a nicer guy." September 25, 1972

Sam Bailey, former Tampa University football coach, discussing a prospect he tried to recruit:
"There's this interior lineman. He's big as a gorilla and strong as a gorilla. Now, if he was smart as a gorilla he'd be fine."
November 6, 1972

Ray Mansfield, former Pittsburgh Steelers center, at a roast for linebacker Jack Lambert:

"I taught Jack a lot—how to tie his shoes, how to brush his fangs."

July 21, 1980

Harold Ballard, owner of the Toronto Maple Leafs, on the timid approach his disappointing team displayed midway through the '74–'75 season:

"You could send Inge Hammarstrom into the corner with six eggs in his pocket and he wouldn't break any of them." December 2, 1974

Mike Patrick, ESPN announcer, upon being introduced as master of ceremonies at the Touchdown Club Awards dinner in Washington, D.C.:
"My broadcast partners are Joe Theismann and Dick Vitale, so I am unaccustomed to public speaking." January 27, 1992

Russ Francis, former NFL tight end, on the hit movie Forrest Gump:
"[It's] the heartwarming story of a simpleminded Southern boy who leads a fantasy sports life. I kind of wish, though, that they had stuck with the original title: "The Terry Bradshaw Story." November 21, 1994

Golfer Mike Donald, when asked why he doesn't have a clothing contract:
"Is it worth $3,000 to look like a jerk?" November 19, 1990

Jack Lemmon, the actor:

"If you think it's hard to meet new people, try picking up the wrong golf ball."

December 9, 1985

Gary Barnett, Northwestern football coach, on the performance of backup quarterback Nick Kreinbrink in the Wildcats' 13–10 loss to Illinois:
"He called a couple of plays we don't have."   October 12, 1998

David Courtney, Los Angeles Kings public relations director, on why he was not preparing a highlights film during the off-season:
"What we have is a highlights slide."   July 21, 1986

Eric Dennis, athletic director at Robert Morris College of Chicago, on how he felt when he learned his school's baseball team had lost to St. Francis of Illinois 71–1:

"I was shocked and surprised—I don't know how we scored a run."

April 15, 1996

Tony Perez, Cincinnati Reds coach, on wire-service reports that pitcher John Smiley was unhappy about his trade from the Pittsburgh Pirates to the Minnesota Twins:

"John Smiley is going to change his name to John Frowny."

April 6, 1992

HEALTH WATCH

Billy Martin, on fracturing a finger hitting a piece of furniture after a bad performance by his Oakland A's:

"I'm getting smarter. I finally punched something that couldn't sue me."
September 6, 1982

Art Donovan, 310-pound former Baltimore Colts defensive lineman, describing himself as a light eater:

"As soon as it's light, I start to eat."
July 14, 1980

Chi Chi Rodriguez, senior golfer, who claims he eats steak every day:

"They say red meat is bad for you, but I never saw a sick-looking tiger."
August 21, 1989

Bill Bain, Los Angeles Rams lineman:

"The actuarial tables show that linemen in this game die at the age of 53. I start collecting my pension at 55. Nice."

October 21, 1985

Larry Dierker, Houston Astros manager, on his move from the team's broadcast booth to the dugout:

"In broadcasting, I was an analyst. By the time I finish managing, I might need one."
April 7, 1997

Jackie Berning, Denver Broncos team nutritionist, on the responses of players who were asked to name the four food groups:

"They didn't hesitate: Wendy's, McDonald's, Pizza Hut and Burger King."
October 1, 1990

Edwin Simmons, Texas tailback, explaining his problems after his third arthroscopic knee surgery in eight months:
"There's no pain when I'm walking, but I'm not a walking back."
September 10, 1984

E.J. Holub, former Kansas City Chiefs linebacker, on his 12 knee operations:
"My knees look like they lost a knife fight with a midget."
August 14, 1978

Ray Perkins, Baltimore Colts rookie, on his operation for a severe skull injury:
"It's just like a knee injury—except I had it in the head."
October 16, 1967

Pat Williams, general manager of the Orlando Magic, describing his job:
"It's like a nervous breakdown with a weekly paycheck."

June 4, 1990

Jim Valvano, North Carolina State basketball coach, on the dental plan at his school:
"We either win or the alumni bash our teeth in."

May 2, 1988

Bill Russell, discussing onetime Boston Celtics teammate Gene Conley, who also pitched for the Boston Red Sox:

"After the season with the Celtics, he said he couldn't pitch for the Red Sox for four weeks because it took him that long to get out of shape."

May 28, 1984

Gordie Howe, asked whether he's ever broken his nose while playing hockey:

"No, but 11 other guys did."

March 2, 1981

Rob DiMaio, Boston Bruins right wing, on undergoing two off-season operations on his nasal passages:
"They had to take a piece of bone out of my head in order to rebuild my nose. It was kind of a pain in the butt." September 21, 1998

Rod Beck, Chicago Cubs closer, contending that his far-less-than-buff physique doesn't make him injury-prone:
"I've never seen anyone on the DL with pulled fat." March 16, 1998

Stewart Granger, Villanova guard, recalling the rough basketball on Brooklyn playgrounds:
"The rule was 'No autopsy, no foul.' " April 4, 1983

Bum Phillips, coach of the New Orleans Saints, after passing a physical examination:
"If I drop dead tomorrow, at least I'll know I died in good health."
November 11, 1985

Bill Fitch, Boston Celtics coach:
"I don't have an ulcer. I'm a carrier. I give them to other people."
February 11, 1980

Lou Duva, manager of heavyweight champion Evander Holyfield, on portly challenger George Foreman:

"Some people say George is fit as a fiddle, but I think he looks more like a cello."   December 10, 1990

Tony DeSpirito, veteran jockey:

"I had a lot of things I wanted to do during my vacation, but instead I just relaxed and got fat. Well, maybe not really fat. I put on a pound."   February 28, 1972

William Perry, the Clemson football team's 6' 3", 305-pound freshman middle guard, talking about his childhood:
"When I was little, I was big."   November 9, 1981

Bubba Paris, San Francisco 49ers offensive tackle, proudly noting that he had slimmed down in the off-season from 377 pounds to 340:
"Now I look like a normal fat human being."   August 20, 1990

Charles Barkley, Houston Rockets forward, on the effects of aging on his 34-year-old body:
"I used to be a Chippendale. Now I'm a Clydesdale."   April 14, 1997

Johnny Bench, baseball Hall of Famer, when asked how he felt about Carlton Fisk's breaking his career record for home runs by a catcher:

"I was thinking about making a comeback, until I pulled a muscle vacuuming."

September 10, 1990

MEDIA
CIRCUS

Bob Costas, NBC sportscaster, on loquacious basketball commentator Dick Vitale:
"Once I didn't speak to him for two months. I didn't think it was right to interrupt him." November 16, 1987

Irving Rudd, boxing publicist, on the oft-heard statement that Howard Cosell was his own worst enemy:
"Not while I'm alive." July 21, 1986

Ken Squier, television commentator, offering advice to colleagues working the NASCAR Coca-Cola 600 for Russian and Ukrainian TV:

"There are only two things you really have to grasp. You have to be able to say, 'There they go' and 'What a wreck!' " June 26, 1989

Michael Jordan, Chicago Bulls guard, when asked his reaction to being named to the NBA all-interview team:

"No comment." June 22, 1992

Bobby Knight, Indiana's former basketball coach, when asked at a luncheon what part of coaching he liked best:
"Dealing with the press. After the demands of a game, my mind needs a rest." January 10, 1983

Skip Caray, Atlanta Braves broadcaster, upon being introduced to Ted Giannoulas, a.k.a. The San Diego Chicken:
"Why did you cross the road?" October 4, 1982

Sean O'Grady, former lightweight champion and USA Network analyst, noting that many boxers go without showers for days before their bouts:
"Talking to a fighter at a weigh-in is like learning to swim. You have to remember to turn and breathe, turn and breathe."   May 15, 1989

Dan Issel, Denver Nuggets broadcaster, anticipating a jump ball between Denver's 5' 10" Michael Adams and Charlotte's 5' 3" Muggsy Bogues:
"This will be the first time the referee drops the ball."
December 31, 1990

Jack Arute, ESPN commentator, when driver Jimmy Means lost a wheel near the end of a NASCAR race in Brooklyn, Mich.:
"You picked a fine time to leave me, loose wheel." September 1, 1986

Jeff Innis, Mets pitcher, complaining about an unflattering newspaper photo of him:
"That picture was taken out of context." April 8, 1991

Darryl Dawkins, Philadelphia 76ers center, just before he took a vow of silence with sportswriters:

"Nothing means nothing, but it isn't really nothing because nothing is something that isn't."

May 22, 1978

Ron Davis, Minnesota Twins pitcher, objecting to a newspaper story in which he was quoted as criticizing the club's management for trading away many of its top players:

"All I said was that the trades were stupid and dumb, and they took that and blew it all out of proportion."

September 20, 1982

Gregg Jefferies, New York Mets second baseman, on why he never tells the press what pitch he hit:
"I might want to hit it again."   November 26, 1990

Larry Nelson, PGA golfer, while playing in a Tour event at Walt Disney World:
"I want to win here, stand on the 18th green and say, 'I'm going to the World Series.' "   November 11, 1991

Hank Stram, dapper ex-NFL coach and current TV and radio color announcer, denying reports that he had 400 suits:
"I'm lucky if I own 200."   February 10, 1982

Chipper Johnson, Southern Methodist University field goal kicker who served as a weekend sportscaster on Dallas television, on being asked his greatest asset as an announcer:

"I dress nice and I don't have any pimples."

June 14, 1971

Lindsey Nelson, who was let off free after being stopped by a traffic cop for speeding:

"I said I was a broadcaster for the New York Mets, and he said, 'Buddy, you've got enough troubles.' "
September 3, 1962

Pittsburgh broadcaster Steve Blass, explaining why Democratic presidential candidate Michael Dukakis, while attending a Pirates-Dodgers game in Los Angeles, remained seated during a Wave:

"It was going to the right."
August 8, 1988

Princess Diana, upon meeting London Monarchs kicker Phil Alexander, who was in full uniform at a charity luncheon to promote the World League of American Football:
"I think I'm underdressed."
May 29, 1991

Mike Schmidt, Phillies third baseman, addressing a Philadelphia sportswriters' banquet:
"Philadelphia is the only city in the world where you can experience the thrill of victory and the agony of reading about it the next day."
February 9, 1981

ALL IN THE FAMILY

*Leon Wood, New Jersey Nets guard,
introducing himself to the team's TV
commentator, Steve Albert:*

"Are you any relation to your brother Marv?"

November 24, 1986

*Curt Schilling, Philadelphia Phillies pitcher, on his less-than-sculpted 6' 4",
234-pound physique:*
"This isn't a body. It's a cruel family joke."   June 9, 1997

*Lisa McCaffrey, wife of Broncos receiver Ed McCaffrey, on Ed's latest
concussion:*
"When he didn't remember our anniversary, I knew he was O.K."
                                                              November 22, 1999

Rick Pitino, Kentucky basketball coach, when asked about one of his team's defensive alignments:

"That's our mother-in-law set—constant nagging and harassment."

February 26, 1990

Chuck Nevitt, North Carolina State basketball player, explaining to coach Jim Valvano why he appeared nervous at practice:

"My sister's expecting a baby, and I don't know if I'm going to be an uncle or an aunt."

January 18, 1982

Lee Smith, St. Louis Cardinals pitcher, on the pressure brought by his reported $7.8 million contract:
"I was born under pressure. My mom wanted a girl." July 30, 1990

Kevin Mitchell, Cleveland Indians outfielder, on why he eats Vick's VapoRub:
"My grandmother told me it was good for colds. It sure blows out those sinuses." May 19, 1997

Jack Elway, San Jose State football coach:
"John Elway is a great football player. He used to be my son. Now I'm his father." January 24, 1983

Donna Horton White, after sinking a 25-foot putt in an LPGA tournament in Deerfield Beach, Fla., while seven months pregnant:
"That putt was so good I could feel the baby applauding."

March 9, 1981

Keith Closs, Los Angeles Clippers rookie center, after missing practices to attend the funerals of his grandmother and his cousin:
"I've apologized, and it won't happen again." November 24, 1997

Dale Berra, Pittsburgh Pirates shortstop and son of noted linguist Yogi Berra, on comparisons between him and his father:

"Our similarities are different."

February 16, 1983

Beth Holtz, wife of former Notre Dame football coach Lou Holtz, when asked about her husband's peripatetic coaching career:
"The first thing we look for in a house is its resale value."

December 23, 1985

Mookie Wilson, Mets outfielder, explaining why he was wed in a ballpark:
"My wife wanted a big diamond."

October 13, 1986

Patti Corzine, wife of Chicago center Dave Corzine, following a Bulls victory over the Philadelphia 76ers, who were playing without Moses Malone:
"I knew something was wrong when Dave came home with no bite marks."

March 12, 1984

Betsy Cronkite, when told that her husband, Walter, an avid sailor and former news anchor, wished to die on a 60-foot yacht with a 16-year-old mistress by his side:

"He's more likely to die on a 16-foot yacht with a 60-year-old mistress."   October 13, 1986

Ilie Nastase, on why he didn't report the loss of his American Express credit card:

"Whoever stole it is spending less money than my wife."
                                                                                      July 31, 1978

Lee Trevino, recalling his boyhood:

"My family was so poor they couldn't afford any kids. The lady next door had me."

July 26, 1971

Candy Davis, wife of relief pitcher Mark Davis, marveling at her husband's new four-year, $13 million contract with the Kansas City Royals:
"You'd think he discovered the cure for cancer or something."

December 25, 1989

Joe Torre, New York Yankees manager and father of an infant daughter, on whether nighttime feedings disturbed his sleep:
"I'm 55 years old. I get up three times a night to go to the bathroom. The baby is on my schedule."

April 29, 1996

Ed Temple, who coached eight women's Olympic track gold medalists during his 38 years at Tennessee State:

"I'm the only man alive whose wife approves of him going around with fast women."
December 18, 1989

Dan Plesac, Milwaukee Brewers pitcher, on a phone conversation with his mother after he gave up a 520-foot homer to the Detroit Tigers' Cecil Fielder:

"I told her, 'Yeah, it barely went out.' I didn't tell her it barely went out of the stadium."
September 30, 1991

Mrs. Laura Quilici, hearing that her son Frank had been made manager of the Minnesota Twins:
"Oh, the poor kid."   December 25, 1972

Fred Akers, University of Texas football coach:
"Football doesn't take me away from my family life. We've always watched films together."   June 4, 1979

Anne Hayes, wife of Ohio State's Woody Hayes, asked if she had ever contemplated divorce:
"Divorce, no. Murder, yes."   September 23, 1974

Lou Henson, Illinois basketball coach, on why he was not recruiting ex–Indiana coach Bob Knight's promising 6' 6" son Pat:
"I didn't want to pay him a home visit."   December 25, 1989

Brad Scott, South Carolina football coach, after his wife, Daryle, broke her left ankle and sprained her right ankle while leaving a game:
"She's probably out for the season."   October 26, 1998

Joe Kocur, New York Rangers right wing, on the previous Friday's fight with his former roommate and still close friend, Bob Probert of the Detroit Red Wings:
"Before, we only fought over who should clean the house."
December 27, 1993

Veronica Fleury, wife of Calgary Flames forward Theo Fleury, after an errant shot from Flames defenseman Zarley Zalapski hit her in the head while she was watching a game:

"Good thing he didn't get me in the teeth, or I'd look just like Theo."

April 1, 1996

Jeanne Austin, mother of 16-year-old tennis star Tracy:

"When Tracy was eight, she would beat the best ladies at the tennis club in California, and then go over to the baby-sitting area and play in the sandbox."

May 21, 1979

Suzanne Martin, wife of Washington Redskins owner Jack Kent Cooke, on whether her husband gets upset if one of his players is injured:

"Certainly. Yes, he does—as if one of our racehorses were hurt."

November 16, 1987

Dick (Digger) Phelps, new Notre Dame basketball coach, on how he got that nickname:

"My father is an undertaker, and I worked for him part time. There were advantages to the job. For instance, while I was dating my wife I sent her flowers every day."

May 24, 1971

OUT OF
BOUNDS

Don King, boxing promoter, citing his credentials to speak to an assembly of Harvard Law School students:
"I've been in more courtrooms than any of you." September 30, 1996

Jay Leno, comedian and, at the time, regular guest host of The Tonight Show:
"Oklahoma's football team has already been ranked 10th in the preseason polls—that's UPI and FBI." March 6, 1989

Don James, University of Washington football coach, on the advantages of having a player named to the Playboy preseason all-star team:
"I like it because it's the one month out of the year my wife lets me buy the magazine." September 10, 1979

Chuck Daly, Detroit Pistons coach and noted clotheshorse, after seeing a $1,300 virgin wool suit in a New York City store:

"I'd rather have something for around $300 from a sheep that fooled around a little."

June 4, 1990

John Elway, Denver Broncos quarterback, on the repeated diagramming in Denver newspapers of his ruptured biceps tendon:

"I just hope I never get kicked in the groin." August 18, 1997

Jay Hilgenberg, Chicago Bears center, on the five quarterbacks his team is bringing to training camp:

"All those quarterbacks feel the same to me." July 13, 1987

Ivan Zamorano, Chile's captain, upon hearing Madonna proclaim him one of the 10 sexiest soccer players at the World Cup:

"She thinks that now, and she has only seen me fully dressed."

June 29, 1998

Elliott Maddox, New York Mets third baseman, describing himself as bilingual:
"I have an off-season vocabulary and a during-season vocabulary."

July 21, 1980

George Perles, Michigan State football coach and renowned malapropist, on women in the locker room:
"I think we probably expose our players to the media as well as anybody."

October 22, 1990

Ron Santo, asked what knowledge manager Leo Durocher imparted to his 10th-place Cubs:
"Well, one thing, we all learned some new words."

October 10, 1966

Woody Widenhofer, Vanderbilt football coach, on what he wanted his team to show against Alabama:

"The kind of confidence that the 82-year-old man had when he married a 25-year-old woman and bought a five-bedroom house next to an elementary school."

September 22, 1997

Harro Esmarch, official of the International Luge Federation, on the IOC's nixing of a unisex doubles luge event:
"Some people's fantasies have no boundaries."   February 23, 1998

Jacques Rogge, International Olympic Committee physician, on what the IOC would do at the 2000 Olympics if Sydney, which had had three outbreaks of drinking-water contamination in the previous year, were to have another during the Games:
"We'll all have to drink whiskey."   September 28, 1998

Barbara Romack, on being named president of the Ladies Professional Golf Association:
"It's the second time I have ever been president of anything. The other was when I was the president of the Sacramento Junior Golf Club. Thirty-five boys and one girl—me. We didn't get much business done, but we had great meetings."　　　　June 14, 1965

Bob Packwood, randy resigning senator and would-be author, on the amount of sex in his potentially profitable diaries:
"A little more than Francis of Assisi and a little less than Wilt Chamberlain."　　　　September 18, 1995

Horace Grant, Chicago Bulls forward on Madonna's statement that she wants to own an NBA team:

"There would be a lot of girlfriends saying, 'No way you're going to that team.' "

April 4, 1994

J.T. Hayes, former sprint car and midget car racer, on the sex-change operation that made him Terri O'Connell:

"I not only wanted to be A.J. Foyt, I wanted to be Marilyn Monroe."

January 26, 1998

Earl Strom, basketball referee, when Elvin Hayes broke the NBA record for career fouls:

"I felt like stopping the game and giving him my whistle."

December 13, 1982

Phillies sportscaster Richie Ashburn, discussing rookie first baseman Dane Iorg:

"The kid doesn't chew tobacco, smoke, drink, curse or chase broads. I don't see how he can possibly make it."

April 25, 1977

LUXURY
BOX

*Jack Buck, St. Louis Cardinals broadcaster, after catching a glimpse of
George Steinbrenner's yacht on Tampa Bay:*
**"It was a beautiful thing to behold, with all 36 oars working in
unison."**
April 6, 1981

*Mike Milbury, New York Islanders general manager, on Paul Kraus, the agent for
free-agent forward Zigmund Palffy, who had spurned several Milbury offers:*
**"It's too bad he lives in the city. He's depriving some small village of
a pretty good idiot."**
November 9, 1998

John McMullen, Houston Astros owner and former limited partner of Yankees boss George Steinbrenner:

"Nothing is more limited than being a limited partner of George's."

May 19, 1980

Pat Williams, Philadelphia 76ers general manager, at a roast of Utah Jazz coach Frank Layden:

"When the list of great coaches is finally read, I believe Frank Layden will be there listening."

July 23, 1984

Syd Thrift, former baseball executive:

"I like to call the American League East the Fortune 500, because its teams are spending a fortune and playing .500." August 6, 1990

Donald Davidson, Houston Astros executive, extolling pitcher Joe Niekro's ability to relax:

"It takes him an hour and a half to watch *60 Minutes*." March 9, 1981

Jay Leno, comedian and host of The Tonight Show:

"The baseball season is under way. Yesterday they threw out the first owner." February 15, 1993

HUMBLE PIE
& SOUR GRAPES

Dave Lemonds, Chicago White Sox pitcher, on the Kansas City Royals' new Tartan Turf ball park:
"It's like playing marbles in a bathtub."   May 14, 1973

Joe Barry Carroll, Golden State's 7-foot center, on what it's like to grow up tall:
"As a kid, I was big for my age. As I got older, I got big for anybody's age."   January 17, 1983

Casey Stengel, asked if Mexico City's altitude bothered his players after the Mexico City Red Devils beat the Mets 6–4:
"Not a bit; we lose at any altitude."   March 16, 1964

Dennis Lamp, Chicago Cubs pitcher, whose pitching hand was badly bruised when Lou Brock caromed a ball off it for his 3,000th hit:
"I guess they'll be sending my fingers to Cooperstown."

August 27, 1979

Joe DiMaggio, reflecting on what his salary might have been in baseball's current free-agent market:
"If I were sitting down with George Steinbrenner and based on what Dave Winfield got for his statistics, I'd have to say, 'George, you and I are about to become partners.'"

February 10, 1982

Al Downing, former Los Angeles Dodger lefthander, who 20 years ago served up Henry Aaron's record-breaking 715th home run, on living with his place in history:

"I never say 'seven-fifteen' anymore. I now say 'quarter after seven.'"

April 18, 1994

Sparky Lyle, now a Texas Rangers reliever, on his Yankees World Series ring:

"I wanted to find out if the diamond was for real, so I cut the glass on my coffee table with it. Then I found out the coffee table was worth more than the ring."

April 2, 1979

Harry Neale, coach of the Vancouver Canucks:
"Last season we couldn't win at home, and this season we can't win on the road. My failure as a coach is that I can't think of anyplace else to play."
February 11, 1980

Bob Patterson, the Chicago Cubs reliever, describing the pitch on which he surrendered a game-winning home run to the Cincinnati Reds' Barry Larkin:
"It was a cross between a screwball and a changeup—a screwup."
May 6, 1996

Dave Stockton, pro golfer, criticizing the Poppy Hills Golf Course in Pebble Beach, Calif., for being unreasonably tough:
"Even the men's room has a double dogleg." January 23, 1989

Bill Bonham, Chicago Cubs rookie pitcher, after walking three, giving up a single and failing to retire any of four St. Louis Cardinals he faced in his first Major League game:
"I guess I was due for a bad outing." April 19, 1971

Bob Rosburg, pro golfer, discussing the Hazeltine National Golf Club course at Chaska, Minn., with its 10 dogleg holes:
"Robert Trent Jones must have laid out the course in a kennel."

May 4, 1970

Mike Flanagan, Baltimore Oriole pitcher:
"You know you're having a bad day when the fifth inning rolls around, and they drag the warning track."

April 20, 1992

Jack Nicklaus, asked how he missed an 18-inch putt:
"The same way you do."

August 22, 1966

R.C. Slocum, Texas A&M football coach, on losing prize recruit Chip Ambres to a $1.5 million Florida Marlins contract:
"I have a lot of rules and no money. Baseball has a lot of money and no rules."
August 24, 1998

Brandy Johnson, gymnast, on shopping for shoes for her size 3 feet:
"It's hard to find heels that don't have Mickey Mouse on them."
July 30, 1990

Lou Brock, after playing in the National Old-Timers' Baseball Classic in Washington, D.C.:
"The real thrill in this game is to finish it."
July 14, 1986

Dan Quisenberry, Kansas City relief pitcher, after receiving the American League Fireman of the Year award:

"I want to thank all the pitchers who couldn't go nine innings, and manager Dick Howser, who wouldn't let them." December 6, 1982

Duffy Daugherty, Michigan State football coach, after center Walt Forman, whose grade average was 3.89 out of a possible 4.0, quit the team to enter medical school:

"We've learned our lesson. We won't recruit anybody that intelligent again." October 17, 1966

Glenn Abbott, Seattle pitcher, on the Mariners' acquisition of sluggers Richie Zisk and Jeff Burroughs:
"We lost a lot of games last year 3–2 and 4–3. Now we'll have a chance to lose 9–8."
March 30, 1981

Jim Dent, senior pro golfer known for his long but not always accurate drives:
"I can airmail the ball, but sometimes I don't get the right address on it."
July 24, 1989

Wilt Chamberlain on Philadelphia coach Alex Hannum's training sessions:
"If I can miss five minutes of one of his practices, I feel like I am adding five years to my life."
October 23, 1967